AF593991

TIGHT HEADS LOOSE BALLS

TIGHT HEADS LOOSE BALLS

MIKE BURTON

ILLUSTRATIONS BY BILL TIDY

Futura
Macdonald & Co
London & Sydney

A Futura Book

First published in Great Britain in 1981 by
Queen Anne Press, A division of
Macdonald & Co (Publishers) Ltd

First Futura edition 1982

ISBN: 0 7088 2213 4

Made by Lennard Books,
The Old School,
Wheathampstead, Herts AL4 8AN

Editor Michael Leitch
Designed by David Pocknell's Company Limited
Production Reynolds Clark Associates Limited
Printed and bound in Yugoslavia by
Mladinska Knjiga, Ljubljana

Futura Publications
A division of Macdonald & Co (Publishers) Ltd
Maxwell House
74 Worship Street
London EC2A 2EN

CONTENTS

PREFACE

Rugby men fall into two groups. They belong either to the squad – that's the men who actually play the game – or to the miscellaneous alickadoos and hangers-on – that's the people who are part of the club set-up, or are administrators or journalists. All these and more are profiled in the pages that follow. We also go to trials and training sessions, on a tour, to the sevens, and finally spend a weekend together at a major international – events which bring out the best, the worst and the typical in both rugby players and supporters.

From the day I left school I have been assessing these types. At first it was an unconscious process, then in time rugby people and their ways impressed themselves more and more firmly on me. My first encounter with adult rugby began in the back yard of a pub called The Fleece. What happened is too tangled a tale to go into here. Consider only the thoughts of my mother.

At about six o'clock in the evening, she had watched her fifteen-year-old son set off happily on his bicycle for his first rugby training session.

Seven hours later, here he was again, lifting his smashed bike from the roof of a total stranger's car. One side of his face was covered in grazes and bruises, the other in lipstick and powder. Thick fumes of alcohol came towards her on the night breeze as he approached, cigarette in hand.

Despite the shock to my mother, on the strength of my showing that evening I was selected two days later as travelling reserve for the 4th XV. I was to discover during my years in rugby that the people and attitudes I met that night exist in rugby clubs everywhere in the world. In this book I have set down a record of those types as I have encountered them.

THE SQUAD

All rugby players regard themselves as the best at what they do. They love to read their names in the paper, and hear small-talk about themselves on radio, TV, in the bar or in the bog – so long as it's complimentary. Their aim in life is to get as far up the rugby ladder as possible. They have little time or respect for any of the committee men in the club, whom they regard as boring old buggers who can't drink pints any more and who will crack down on them with disciplinary measures when a hotel door gets broken on tour. In truth those boring old buggers were twice as bad in their playing days as the present lot and although today's players do not know it yet, they are tomorrow's committee men.

Players take the game very seriously even at the lowest level. Clubs now have regular squads and fitness sessions. They see rugby as the most important thing in their lives. They tell themselves that they enjoy a quiet drink after the match with the other team but never get pissed or play childish bar-games. Well, not too often anyway.

The position you play in a rugby team is largely decided by your own physical make-up. For example: short fat men – front row; tall slim men – locks or No. 8; fast fat men – flankers; short fat fast men – scrum-halves. Backs or three-quarters can be classified as a collection of medium-paced has-beens or going-to-bes between 5ft 6in and 6ft 1in who can make the occasional tackle. Now let's run an eye more slowly down the team sheet.

THE FULL-BACK

First on the team list, he is tall, usually quite athletic and has little vees in the sides of his extra short shorts. He always figures in Press reports because he takes the goal kicks. In the 58 – 3 defeat he will be the only name from our team on the score sheet. This player is particularly cunning in defence. A favourite last-ditch ploy is to hang back in a corner-flag try situation and then launch into a valiant diving tackle without actually making contact with the try-scorer. He then lies still, face down, for a few seconds to register his disgust at the pathetic defensive play of the men in front of him. He is seen at his best in the end of season charity match when it doesn't matter if you win or lose. He will not only kick every attempt at goal but also score tries taking the final pass from the winger who has beaten the cover anyway. He has that unforgiveable knack of missing the last-minute penalty kick when it really counts and then walking back to the half-way line mumbling about cross-winds and failing light.

LEFT-WING

Just up from the Colts, the team's fastest man. This glue-sniffing flyer retains his perfect hairdo at the final whistle; he has a degree in Maths but no footballing brains at all. He has a dashing sports car parked near

GLUE
BRAIN
GUTS
MAZAROTTI
OWNERS CLUB

the clubhouse but on the field he is completely gutless. He can be heard regularly complaining about his opposite number being left with an overlap. Disregard all he says; he would not have tackled him anyway. This man always retires early, say at twenty-six or twenty-seven, and having qualified at something clever he becomes the perfect alickadoo. Always talks about what happened in his day. Such men often aspire, later in life, to become judges, magistrates or local government officials. Although an eloquent after-dinner speaker, he is openly disliked by the forwards who have pet-named him 'Bumper' because of his pathetic attempts at tackling. He has been trying to introduce the classical three-quarter play he knew in his public-school days but our lads prefer the non-classical drop-everything-and-rely-on-the-forwards style which they have been using since the war. He dislikes dressing-room funnies about him being posher than us, and argues that he represents the Average Englishman – standing somewhere between the Cambridge Blue and the Coventry car worker.

LEFT-CENTRE

Can't run, catch or pass but is in the side for his devastating tackling. He's supposed to be the ideal foil for a fast side-stepping centre. He's a top crash man from twenty-five yards out. Is respected by the forwards as the hardest man in the team. He has no regard for his own safety let alone the safety of the opposite centre. He is a very good tourist and will often attract back to the team's hotel a good-looking woman and several of her grotty mates to be molested by the front row. He never becomes annoyed when he fails to score himself. He's the player's representative on the committee and is currently locked in conflict with the senior administrators over increased bar prices and match-fee reductions. He lists among his pastimes rugby, racing and beer in that order. Women slot in somewhere behind snooker, cards and TV. Thinks most outside-halves are ponces and all props unsung heroes. He loves to recount the story of his early playing days battling it out in the mud on a wet Wednesday afternoon in the middle of winter. He's not at all interested in committee work and after retirement will only be seen at the annual dinner.

RIGHT-CENTRE

The right-centre has blistering pace but is a consistent hospital-passer and a total coward in the tackle. Often a doctor by profession. Feigns a hamstring injury and leaves the field if the going gets really rough. Broke the club record for dropped goals two seasons running. Nasty rumour that he had dropped them in fright after the opposition centre had farted within ten yards of him. This man is completely trustworthy, always punctual on match days, never been known to miss training, enjoys touch rugby, always buys his rounds, and when watching one of the club's other XVs is always asked to hold the valuables box. His two main aims in life are to finish a cup game and to become treasurer. He is the president's son and is constantly arguing with the outside-half over who should call the moves. Sulks when he is the man out on a miss-move and is described by the Welsh members of the club as a typical English club player because he arrives for the match in a suit even when he hasn't come from work. Annoyed every other member of the team when he joined last year by being chosen for the first team without playing in the club trials or 2nd XV. He came here with experience in the Hospitals' Cup Competition, and went straight into our 1st XV on the strength of one appearance in the 'Varsity Match and two dropped goals playing for Combined Services against a touring circus.

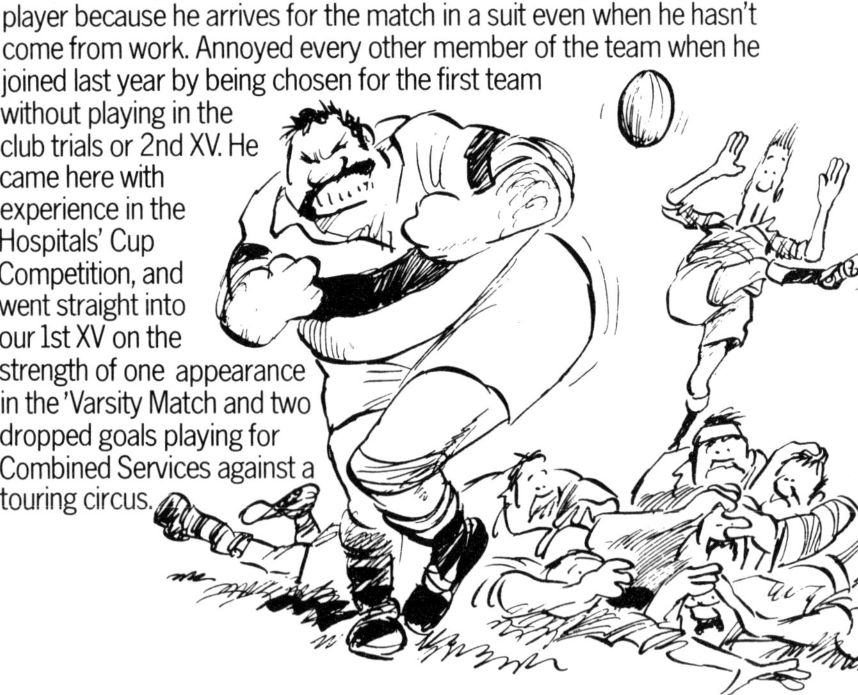

RIGHT-WING

No pace at all, nicknamed 'Dobbin' by his team-mates, dynamite from ten yards out, tackles anything early. Would be the leading try scorer if he could catch. Diabolical dress sense – never gets the girl. Yearns to be a forward and is prepared to go down to the third team to learn the trade properly. Currently completing a one-year suspension for drinking and driving, he rides a bike to and from games and training, claiming you can't be done for riding a bike while drunk in charge. Still unemployed two years after the local brewery closed down but stopped drawing social security after a good run on the horses. No interest in committee work but half an eye on the groundsman's job.

OUTSIDE-HALF

Slightly smaller than the scrum-half and would like to have played there but has no pass to speak of. Anyway he considers himself safer ten yards further from the forwards. He sometimes gets the same cheap publicity as the full-back by sharing the goal-kicking duties. If unable to score, make a break or leave some other mark of distinction on the game, he will attempt several drop-kicks in a desperate attempt to retain the respect of his colleagues. He is the team smoothie and works as a representative, chatting up receptionists all day and playing with himself all night. He stands faithfully next to his girlfriend at home games talking about the mortgage rates and property values. He drinks two halves before driving round to her house for tea. On away games and tours he turns into a sex maniac and teams up with the hooker who will always have the ugly one of the two. Like all up-and-coming youngsters he considers himself world-class and probably will be if she lets him develop. Can kick with both feet, has pace, sees all opposition as fairies and spends the twelve months after we've won the local derby wise-cracking about the last victory, eg 'Why don't you combine with the Rest of the World and see if you can beat us?' This quietly amusing lad would never admit it but he is also very sensitive and visibly hurt by suggestions that anything could be wrong with our club or the way we play. This fierce pride makes him a great competitor. He finds it hard to accept defeat, particularly when the other team have scored more points.

SCRUM-HALF

Short, with a king-size personality, but underneath he has a bit of a complex about his height. He either hides this complex behind his huge extrovert nature or it manifests itself in sudden bursts of aggression against big forwards or a sharp retort to some harmless comment by a taller team-mate. Always wears cuban heels at the piss-up. Never talks to tall women. He works successfully in any job that involves giving instructions to the staff. The same quality makes him a great captain. He enjoys barking his orders to eight big forwards. Answers to the name of 'Corgi'. Has all the grit in the world. Will take the bad ball with the good without ever complaining. Yearns to be taken seriously and no act of bravery on the field is too much in his drive to achieve this. He never wins at cards and for the past two years has been trying to cultivate a moustache which still resembles a thin eye-brow. Recently he applied for a job in the prison service but was turned down because of a rule about minimum height. Has just returned from a tour of Fiji with an invitation All Star team, and regards our forwards as soft because they wear boots.

THE FRONT ROW

The front-row forwards are generally reckoned to be the dumbest members of the team. Anyone who does not play there cannot understand how they can possibly enjoy it. In his heart of hearts every front-row forward knows that if he were clever enough or fast enough to play in any other position he would. The front row like to be considered as a team. After each match they can be seen standing together at the bar discussing the niceties of front-row play. The props are joint holders of the Punch of the Year award and the hooker is firm favourite for the Provoker of the Decade trophy.

Together they take credit for the two strikes against the head that they had on their line or the push-over try that was disallowed. The hooker graciously accepts responsibility for the one they lost against the head, telling the loose-head: 'It was my timing that was at fault'. But eight pints later, and now standing in separate pubs talking to some ignorant three-quarter or woman, the hooker claims he struck those balls against the head despite the props and how could that loose-head be so bloody

SORRY MATE!

clumsy as to kick it to them. The loose-head expounds his theory about the bad positioning of the hooker and the tight-head sniggers that it is he who is keeping the hooker in the side with his dazzling footwork.

Collectively the front row are tremendous value to the team. They are invariably the best singers, they drink any slops bought for them by anybody, without complaint, including bar dregs after closing time. They are always caught when making an Indian or Chinese restaurant run-out and made to pay up. They also provide the team comedian who will exploit the funny side of most situations. They are long-suffering, uncomplaining souls whose main off-the-field use is to talk to the ugly one while the outside-half is giving her mate one in the back seat of the bus in the car park. Front rows are so used to taking stick from each other that they don't know when they have had a good hiding. The prop will never admit that he has lost the battle and if the scrum is low he will say he wanted it to go low, if it's high he'll say it should be high. He will tell everyone about his good days, never about his bad days. He only cares about the comfort of his hooker. Although they like to win a game, front rows don't mind losing provided they win the scrums.

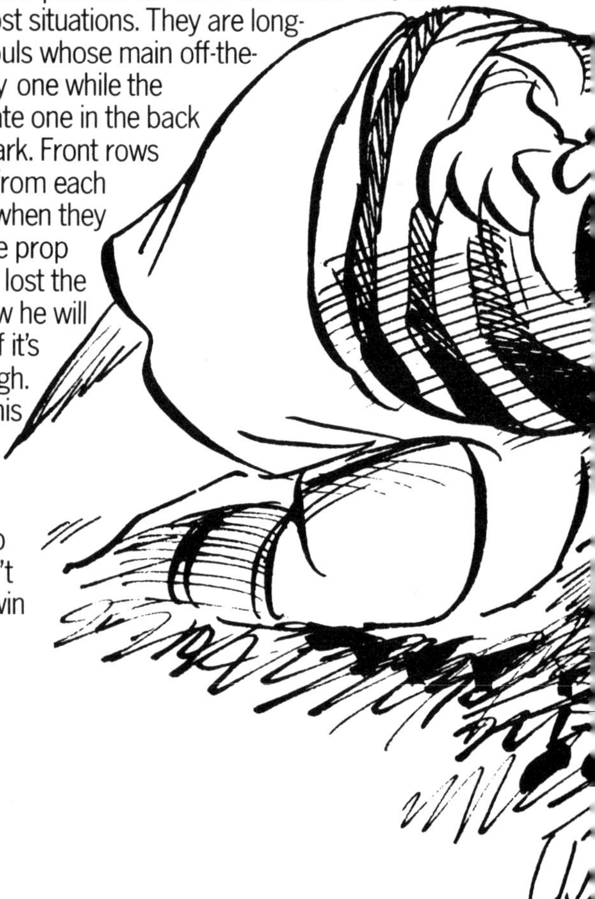

GOLDEN
KNOCKER
RESTAURANT
£66:40
VAT)

LEFT-LOCK

Often falls between two stools. Too tall for a prop and not big enough to make a decent lock-forward. Consequently he stands at No. 2 in the line-out. Says he prefers a fast flat throw to a slow lobbed one because the latter gives his inferior opposite number a chance to impede our hero's brilliant jump. In fact our No. 2 jumper cannot get any higher than six inches off the ground so a fast flat ball is his only hope of winning anything at all. He always blames the thrower when losing a line-out. On the other hand he is an excellent scrummager and regularly will be heard asking his prop: 'How's that? Is that enough? How's the push, kid?' He knows full well that the prop will grunt for everyone to hear: 'Great, keep it going'.

He is usually a bit of a sorter-outer, taking it upon himself to issue warnings to the other pack. These usually involve a pointed finger or a psych-out stare or snarl. In extreme cases he will utter threats like: 'Don't go down on the ball, will you', or 'Alright, you'll have it in a minute'. Occasionally he actually hits someone, making sure it is in full view of the spectators and then racing for the anonymity of the next ruck. If the player he hits requires attention our hero will trot back across the field to ask if he is OK, hoping the bloke will think it was not him who did it in the first place.

He talks a great game in the bar. Should have had a cap but never made the Trials. He is totally dominated by his wife and has fantasies about the rest of the team's wives and girlfriends. Always buys *Playboy* on an away trip but slips it into a single player's kit-bag before going home to face the wife. He is known to the lads as 'Groper', is a builder by trade and supervised the building of the clubhouse.

RIGHT-LOCK

The middle jumper. Tall, lean, about 6ft 4in. Needs much more weight, can't scrummage, brilliant line-out jumper but has no bottle at all. This man, because of his superior height and physical presence, attracts all kinds of female attention. He is the hero of the tea ladies and various other clubhouse women. Despite the attention of these ladies he never actually takes advantage of any of them and on away trips can be seen

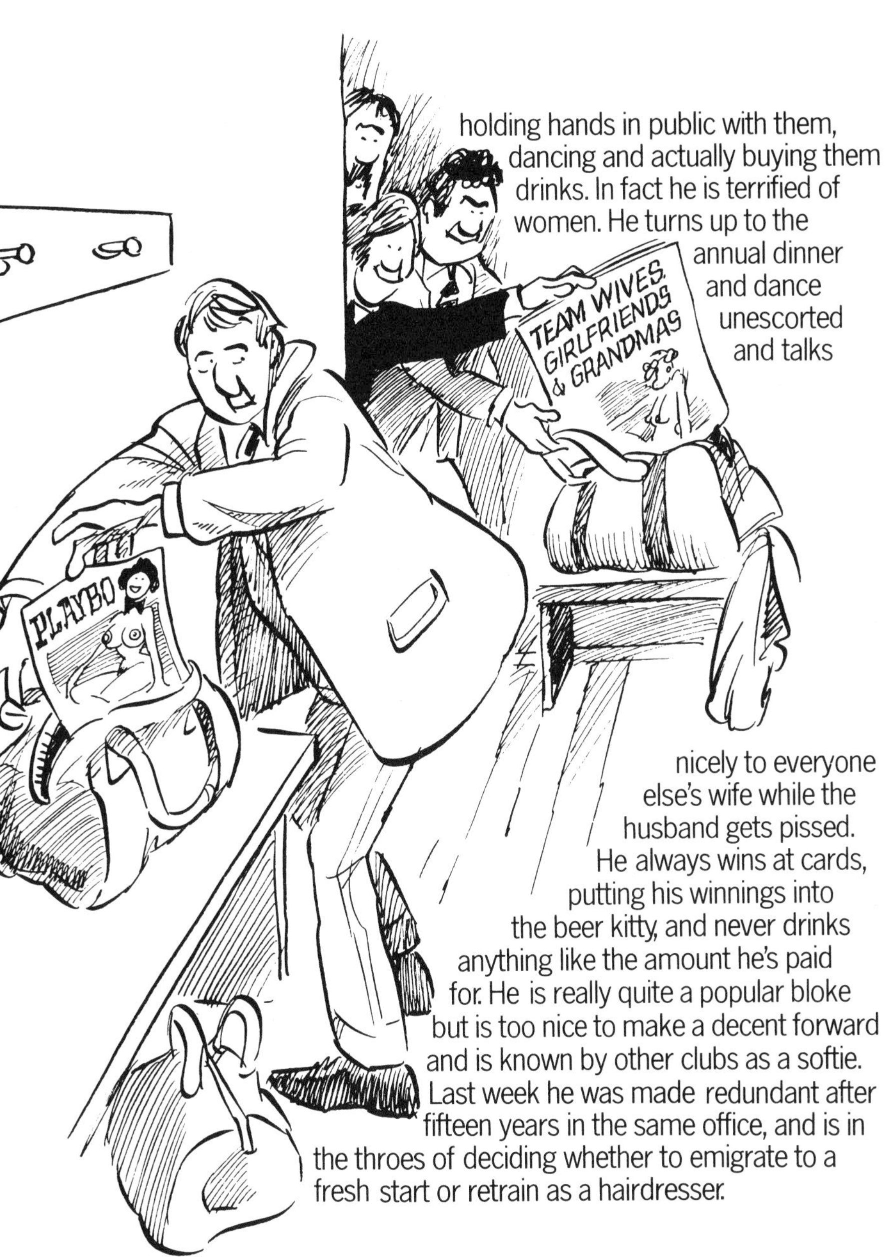

holding hands in public with them, dancing and actually buying them drinks. In fact he is terrified of women. He turns up to the annual dinner and dance unescorted and talks nicely to everyone else's wife while the husband gets pissed. He always wins at cards, putting his winnings into the beer kitty, and never drinks anything like the amount he's paid for. He is really quite a popular bloke but is too nice to make a decent forward and is known by other clubs as a softie. Last week he was made redundant after fifteen years in the same office, and is in the throes of deciding whether to emigrate to a fresh start or retrain as a hairdresser.

I'D LIKE EIGHTEEN OTHER CHINESE RUNOUTS AND A STRIP TO BE TAKEN INTO CONSIDERATION

OPEN-SIDE WING-FORWARD

He is a kamikaze player. He dives into anything or anyone. He has the biggest heart in the team and is frightened of no-one. Unbeaten in street fights and bar brawls, he has pace and goes eight minutes flat-out – never spares himself. The open-side is a flash, brash, screw-anything young man and performs all the team's strips and tricks – like driving the team bus away at 2.30 in the morning or drinking two pints of beer in eight seconds flat. He is always first out during a Chinese or Indian run-out and when caught by the police always puts up a good enough fight to see him before the court on Monday morning. He never pays match fees or subs and rarely buys his round at the bar but is still highly popular and the man all the other members of the team would like to be.

Always plays with his socks rolled down and is currently on a course of treatment for genital rash.

BLIND-SIDE FLANKER

Formerly an open-side, but after a bad injury which affected his pace about the field he moved to blind-side. Has recently started courting a local girl and thinking of getting a job. Since moving to blind-side he has not given away a single penalty for late tackles or going over the top. Has been around long enough to devise his own back-row moves, but is happy to make his colleagues look good while he acts as the foil. Still enjoys a drink. Goes home early after seven quick pints. Occasionally on away matches he reverts to his old self: kicks their scrum-half up in the air and claims that we won because they broke down at half-back. In their clubhouse, the game won, he hits the piss with the open-side but has to spend twice as much as he would have done as the thirsty open-side is skint. When really pissed he confides to everyone his deep love and affection for his new steady. If he'd met her earlier, he claims, he would be a different man. Looks like he could end up coaching.

NO. 8

Tall, slim, good-looking. Not the fastest man in the team but the fittest. Every club has a team donkey and this is him. He dominates the end of the line-out, plays a little loosely, throws the occasional one-handed pass but does his share of covering. Generally speaking a one-hundred per-center. Was a good bloke until he got married last year to one of those whose philosophy, until she got him, was 'I want to take an interest in his sport'. Now she does her level best to get him into retirement before some other young lady hears the bar-room banter about his enormous hampton. No-one will stand next to him in the shower. He is always first in, lathers up his show-piece then stands for a full thirty minutes delighting in the gasps from those who have not seen it before and various curt comments like: 'Christ! Has that got heart and lungs?' The No. 8 will slowly drift away from rugby, completely drained by that good looking but dominating wife who is already turning him into a master carpenter-cum-painter and decorator. Known as 'Snake' by his team-mates.

REPLACEMENTS

Most teams will have two replacements to cover in case of injury for the fifteen men actually on the field. One replacement is a three-quarter and one is a forward.

THE REPLACEMENT THREE-QUARTER

He will trot out right after the team looking fitter than anyone actually playing. He is wearing a beautiful modern tracksuit and does physical jerks and stretches before taking his seat on the bench. He makes intelligent comments throughout the game. Loves a stoppage as this is his opportunity to sprint up and down the touchline in full view of everyone. He is always complimentary about the people he is covering for and never criticizes anyone playing that day, while in his heart of hearts he thinks he is better. Was a schoolboy international fifteen years ago and is still trying to establish himself at senior level.

THE REPLACEMENT FORWARD

This man walks out thirty yards behind the team, head down, shin pads in his hand. He wears a dirty old sweater and a different-coloured track-suit bottom, and mumbles about 'that prick they picked instead of me'. Takes his seat on the bench immediately instead of warming-up with the rest of the team – in fact he refuses to warm-up. When asked by the coach to put on his pads and start warming-up and stretching because someone is down, he will snap back: 'Told you he was a fairy. Shouldn't be out there in the first place.' After the match he will talk about nothing but the diabolical performance of the man who played instead of him and how he is going to get him in training next Tuesday. He knows all the rugby songs but is never happy enough to sing them. Recently played as A N Other in a Rugby League trial and was offered £2,000 to stay in Union.

THE TEAM HARD MAN

Because of the number of high-speed collisions in which he is involved, the hardest man of the team is either a centre or open-side flanker. But, over the years, the legend of the team hard man has belonged to one of the front five. He is a senior forward who never wears a gum-shield and has little more to offer than his physical presence as a frightener to opposition teams who know him and his big right hand. He loves his tough-guy tag and will go to all sorts of lengths to protect it. He is a habitual stiff-arm tackler and is well thought of by all his team-mates as being 'our heavy artillery man'. When telling his tales, whether in the dressing-room or in the bar, he puts on an innocent face and tries to justify his bad deed for the day, explaining how their bloke hit our scrum-half first and how 'I warned him at the two previous line-outs, just to be fair to him'. What really happens is that our hard man will pick out someone in their pack whom he feels he has a good chance of beating anyway and when the opportunity presents itself he throws his big right. Or, when the victim is on the ground, he will run all over him pausing midway through the run to stamp firmly on some part of his anatomy, passing it off later by saying: 'Well, he was lying on it. That will teach him to get off it'.

The same line will be taken in the scrums. He will always claim that their prop bit our hooker. Logical reasons do not matter to our hard man; his greater need is for someone to help him enhance his reputation. He feels really upset if he is not talked to at least twice by the referee and loves to hear people talk about the day he was sent off. These men rarely take a shot at anyone they suspect might beat them – think of the shame! But if they do concede a black eye or facial cut they wear it proudly all night in the bar, and answer to any comment about the injury: 'Ah, but I had him back.' Even if the black eye was sustained bumping into one of his own players he would take glory from it, swearing it was done by 'that dirty bastard I laid out two minutes from time.'

Never worry about this hard man for he is all wind and piss. He is hopeless in a bar-room brawl, and cries at sentimental films and songs. He hasn't missed a game since joining the club fifteen years ago, and will not accept medical attention on the field for fear someone may think he is going soft.

THE INTERNATIONAL PLAYER

He is the pick of the bunch. Young children look up to him, old men admire and respect him. Becoming an international has turned working-class boys into building-society managers, and miners into sports-shop owners, overnight. Playing international rugby is the most important achievement in any player's life because for ever after he will be labelled ex-Springbok, former-Welsh-this or former-Irish-that. A New Zealand journalist once wrote that if the Prime Minister of New Zealand died and had once been an All-Black the headline would read not 'Prime Minister Dies' but 'ALL-BLACK DIES.'

Of course, this special man enjoys all that goes with being a star. Dinner invitations, top of everyone's party list, he may well become an accomplished after-dinner speaker, taking confidence from the wonderful response he receives from an audience waiting on his every word, not because of what he says but because of who he is. He may even become so good at speaking at these functions that he finds a fat envelope slipped into his pocket containing more than just expenses. It is difficult

for him to turn his back on commercially exploiting the situation in which he finds himself. Sports-equipment companies will not only supply his boots but may well tuck into them a few crisp banknotes. Indeed when playing in an international, and mindful of the presence of both equipment manufacturers and selectors, he finds it difficult to decide whether to dive about flashing his number to the selectors or his distinctive boot-markers to the manufacturers.

By far the most pleasurable and ego-boosting way for him to earn a backhander is the Sunday-afternoon match against a junior team celebrating a centenary or clubhouse opening. He cannot fail to look absolutely marvellous when he and his international colleagues play against a team of also-rans. Afterwards he and the other internationals will modestly sip free beer and revel in the admiration of the locals. He will sign a few books for dads who always say: 'It's for my son.'

The international player is at his very best in his own clubhouse. Above the bar hangs his photograph and the international jerseys that he presented to the club. He is only human and loves to be in the environment where he is instantly recognized as a hero and where the locals love to hear him reminisce about the big games he has played or the major tours he has been on.

THE COLT

Described officially as an Under-18 player, he has the whole world at his feet. He is still a little self-conscious about his appearance and is just sprouting a few pubic hairs. Spends all his spare money on pimple cream and *Playboy* magazine, not caring at all if he does go blind. He has yet to discover the joys of someone pissing in his pocket as he stands shoulder-to-shoulder on the East Terrace at the Arms Park or the disappointment of getting her tanked up, taking her to his room and then finding that he's had too much himself. He still believes that rugby is all that matters and that missing a tackle is a bigger disaster than the sinking of the *Titanic*. He is an attentive listener to all the coach says and would rather die than lose. His dressing-room small-talk revolves around Betty's tits or Sylvia's pubics – a good healthy lad. One of tomorrow's men. Look after him.

THE GOLDEN OLDIE

And so we come to the end of our playing days. It is a traumatic experience but most take the view that it is sensible to come to terms with it as soon as possible. Not so the golden oldie. He is a quite recent innovation. He may have to qualify for certain teams by being over thirty-five or forty, or even over fifty. He is, in the main, a happy old boy reliving the days of his youth. He will put himself down for the correct age group, turn up at the kick-off and enjoy himself, although he will be walking long before the end.

Occasionally, however, a crafty golden oldie will appear on the scene. He will take the whole thing far too seriously. He will train himself silly weeks before the game and then turn up with that casual haven't-given-the-game-a-thought air and play in a group of oldies who are much less fit and much older than he is. This crafty sort only play to make themselves look better than they really are. They love to hear the touchline mumblings of: 'My word, he's still handy isn't he'. Don't worry about this villain; if there is any justice in the world, he will fall up the steps going into the dressing-room and break his leg, or be beaten up by the wife when he gets home.

THE RETIRED PLAYER

Here is a man that can be separated from the committee man and the general alickadoo as someone who will think he is a player until he dies. He loves to stand with today's players in the bar and talk as all players do about the shortcomings of the committee. Immediately after retirement he will not miss a match but as time goes on his interest diminishes until he turns up only for the occasional big game or a game against a club that has one of his contemporaries on the committee so that he can reminisce. His philosophy is that he will never criticize a player in the way that he was criticized when he played, but after a few pints he will be talking of certain of today's players who wouldn't have had a look-in when he was on the field.

He watches internationals on the telly, and comments knowledgeably to his immediate family. He regrets bitterly the day he became a non-player and occasionally measures how past it he really is by playing in some gash game on a Sunday morning. He will go for the odd road run but always alone and he quietly accepts that he has had it as far as serious rugby is concerned. Refuses to stand for the committee as he would not wish to be considered one of them.

TRIALS AND TRAINING

t the beginning of each year, a bunch of young and not-so-young hopefuls arrive for the trial match. Beware the thirty-two-year-old arriving from some overseas station claiming that he can play outside-half or hooker; he is obviously a hooker who thinks he can fulfil his ambition to play outside-half while keeping his options open should his new team-mates rumble him. The trial rarely means anything – maybe one or two new men get into the first team each year. A sensible selector knows that an average club man will always look good in a trial when marked by a dummy. One such unfortunate is the young lock that arrives for the trial wearing spectacles as thick as milk bottles and is a white-stick case as soon as he takes them off. He is completely outplayed by a thirty-nine-year-old prop just filling in as lock, and when the frustration sets in our trialist throws a punch only to hit the old prop in the knee cap; the blow damages his hand and finally he takes a place in the twelfth team when returning from injury in mid-season.

Nevertheless new trialists should always be made welcome; if you find one good player in ten it will have been worth it. Whether or not the same can be said for the international or area team trials is arguable. The enthusiasm of the young pretender on having heard of his selection for an international trial is dampened when he finds he is playing outside a non-passing centre, a grub-kicking outside-half and a scrum-half whose pass has been accurately described as a five-yard lob. In these circumstances the trialist can be forgiven for contemplating some form of gimmickry. Even here a three-quarter's options are limited. A forward can take the selectors' eye with a white scrum cap or large headband-cum-sweatband daubed with tomato sauce to give the impression that he is bleeding profusely from a severe head wound but is tough enough to continue.

The secret of trial success is to make your bid for stardom as near the Press box as possible. It doesn't matter how many other things you do wrong on the other parts of the field, the Press are probably not watching and if they are they would not know you had done something wrong anyway. The scribes have to back someone, preferably someone new to big-time trials so that they can claim they tipped him for the top when he was a nobody. But whatever happens on the field the real trial starts in the bar thirty minutes after the final whistle. Just feed as many technical titbits as you are able to the loitering Press gang. They cannot let you know they do not understand what you are talking about so they nod knowledgeably. They will further your cause in tomorrow's columns. If you have had a real stinker of a match, tell them you were playing to orders and they will not only write copy supporting your case but openly criticize the selectors for stifling your flair. Selectors read all things to do

with the trials in the hope that they may even be mentioned themselves as being 'not pleased' or 'very impressed'. The player's name that keeps popping up will eventually be selected no matter what happened in the trials.

Selection at schoolboy level is even more of a lottery, for the schoolboy who does not have a master on the selection committe has no chance at all. The successful gamesmaster could double as a horse trader, wheeling and dealing with the other selectors until he gets as many of his men into the team as he can. For example: 'You pick my full-back, I'll pick your winger. You pick my prop and I'll pick your hooker.' This haphazard lottery-type selection is probably the reason why a very large percentage of schoolboy internationals are never any good once they start shaving.

THE COACH

Very few coaches have played rugby at the highest level or been particularly good players. They see success at coaching as a way of expressing all that they feel they should have done in their own careers. Most of the players respect their man and do as they are told. But the player-coach partnership has all the disadvantages of marriage without the advantage of a sexual relationship – we hope – and a boring sort of marriage that is. At club level this apathy or boredom sets in as familiarity grows between the coach and the players. The coach's impact may then diminish over a period of months or years until he is considered by some players to be no more than a baggage man who has read a lot of books or a sponge man who has suddenly acquired great tactical knowledge.

It is much easier to coach an area team, or a provincial or international one, that you only meet a limited number of times a year; even the worst coach can then appear fresh and interesting to the players. Coaches have won fame for winning this cup or that merit table. But a coach is only as good as his players, although very few of them accept that. You can tell a team of dummies the right thing all day and still win nothing. Successful or not, coaches are here to stay. They give their services free – to boys, colts, juniors and seniors – and are on the whole good for the game. When asked to choose between their wives and rugby they always choose their wives. By profession they are teachers.

THE TRAINER

Is most in evidence in the pre-season training grind. Works out ridiculous schedules like hill-running or commando courses. Aged between thirty-five and forty-five, has done some sort of military service, or has been to physical-jerks college. He will amaze everyone with his own fitness. He can do everything he asks you to do but quicker. He loves hearing the lads complain about how hard a taskmaster he is. He is usually less active in the second half of the season but can become busy around April if the first team have a good cup run and suddenly appear to be more committed than before.

Our trainer never smokes but drinks occasionally. He would love to womanize but fears losing the respect of his players. He never argues with the coach but thinks he knows more and should have the job. Has a profound dislike for top players who defy the laws of nature by smoking, drinking, never training, womanizing then playing brilliantly. He loves to run onto the field with the sponge on big match days, in full view of a large crowd. He retired three years ago after losing an eye on tour. Has been known to drop his glass eye into unsuspecting visitors' beer or slip it between bread and offer it to one of the other team's committee men. Nick-named 'Cyclops'.

TRAINING

Most clubs train a couple of times a week, and play on Saturdays. Players attach varying degrees of importance to the matter of physical fitness. During the month of August the captain, no matter how bad he was at training before he became captain, is busy contacting his team and getting those first sessions under way.

Some captains will take responsibility for the physical well-being of their team themselves. Others rely on the help of a specialist coach or trainer like ours – Cyclops.

...15-16.. C'MON, LADS..
TAKE YOUR
BREATHERS
ON THE WAY
DOWN..
17-18..

The first Monday in August arrives, and although everyone at the Annual General Meeting was told to be there, only seven of the fifty-five playing members turn up. One is the team captain, three are second-team players, two are fifth-team players and the other is an overweight committee man bent on losing a few pounds. Cyclops is furious, and all set to take it out on the seven individuals who at least have been decent enough to turn up.

'OK, lads. Start lapping.'

The bunch complete a first circuit of the field, and the committee man pulls up with hamstring trouble. After two more laps, both fifth-team players have brought up their tea and are heading towards the dressing-room.

'Right, hold it there,' Cyclops addresses the four people left in the bunch. 'At least you'll have a full hour's session under your belt. And now, twenty press-ups. In the press-up position. Are you ready, be. . .gin!'

All four complete the exercise, and the session is six minutes old. 'On your feet and trotting, please.' That monotonous round-the-field running, that saps the mind as much as the body, is killing Corgi. But, as first-team captain, he must show that he can do it. Just then, a couple of car-loads pull into the car-park and the trainer's eyes light up. Nine more for training, and six of them are first-teamers.

'OK, lads, just play touch between you while I get the late-comers out of the dressing-room.'

Apart from the fact that the warm-up has been too much, and that two-a-side would look pretty silly, the four on the field haven't got a ball. No-one says anything, in case Cyclops gives them something else to do.

Cyclops leads his nine new trainers out of the dressing-room, plus the two that spewed ten minutes ago and the committee man, although he is limping badly.

'A couple of laps to warm up, you lot, and then we'll go into a circuit.'

Those two laps expose all nine newcomers, with the exception of Dobbin who has been training since last season and is in top condition. The circuit is murderous. Twenty press-ups, twenty burpees, twenty sit-ups, twenty star-jumps – 'Four times lads, please' – followed by a one-and-a-half-mile road run to the nearest gradient. Cyclops, glinting, smiling, stands at the bottom.

'OK, lads. Ten sprints up the gradient. Take your breathers on the way down. Then we'll run back to the training-ground and we'll get some practice against the tackling bags. Anyone finishing behind me gets extra press-ups.'

He really is enjoying this, and has a big smile on his face as we start into the press-ups. The only man to beat him back is Dobbin, and while half-a-dozen complete their penalty press-ups, the captain goes out in his car to locate those lost en route. As dusk falls, the group make their way back to the clubhouse, bundle up their kit and go straight home. No-one, except the coach, stays for a drink.

NO TRAINING –
NO GAMES...
AND THAT INCLUDES
SPACE INVADERS!

Weeks go by. The attendance figure rises with the fitness level. Most of the lads have returned from their holidays and a rumour is going round that the coach is to introduce a policy of 'no training, no games'.

The last session before the first match. Still three members of the first team have not been seen at training. The coach has been having half-hour practices after the basic training and is not happy. 'I need more time to work with them', he says. 'So from next week we'll do only half an hour on fitness and then coaching and practical work for another hour.'

A row breaks out between the trainer and the coach. It is resolved with each getting three-quarters of an hour. To the lads themselves it makes no difference. It hurts just as much to do practical work as it does to get fit. But they are most concerned that the missing three will get into the first team without having to suffer any of the pain that has been inflicted on them.

D-Day approaches. The teams for the first Saturday are put up on the notice-board. The three who have not done a single training session are included: Snake, Groper and Bumper. Threats of resignation and shouts of 'Fix!' rebound around the clubhouse.

'Just a minute, just a minute', calls the coach. The captain's standing on his left, the trainer on his right. 'We are informed that all three of these players have been training throughout the summer, and we are prepared to take them at their word as they are established first-team players.'

Muffled laughs and jeers from the rest of the players. But no-one actually complains. The trio in command wander to the bar, praying that the missing men show up well on Saturday. The coach mumbles: 'At least we're at home. They never play bad at home, do they?' No-one replies.

Comes Saturday, and the game, and everyone's worst fears are realized. Bumper gets through the match, but he is so bad that his opposite number goes up to him and asks if he'd like to retire to save himself further punishment. Snake and Groper collide with each other four yards from touch and near the half-way line, and in front of everyone they begin retching and spewing as no fit man can do. Neither finishes the game.

We lose heavily and Cyclops gives the coach a heavy I-told-you-so look. In the dressing-room afterwards the three give their solemn promise that none of them will miss training again this year.

PLAYING THE GAME

veryone belongs to a club. Clubs have their own identity and special character. They hold trials, enter the sevens tournament, they go on tour and occasionally they have a weekend away as a bunch with the boys on the beer. All those things, however, should be considered as the icing on the cake. The first thing to do is to find fifteen players each week to get out onto the field and represent them. The average small club or second class team has to struggle about from this team to that school to find its men. Later of course some of the players will graduate to the big fashionable clubs with grandstands and match programmes and people paying to watch. But let's first of all go back to that very first night we were telephoned by the club begging us to play....

It's 10.30 on a Friday night, the telephone rings and we are informed by the team secretary that because of a brilliant performance in a training session we attended three weeks ago we have been honoured with selection as a prop-forward for tomorrow's match, which thankfully is at home. That feeling of being needed fades a little as the caller bleats on about players being married on Saturdays and taking half the team to the piss-up. How to get out of this? is the first reaction. 'There must be some mistake,' we say, 'I am a winger.'

The reply comes down the line: 'You've got to start somewhere, son. This will be good experience for you. We will be changing at the Nag's Head and driving to the ground after, so see you at 12.30.'

Five past one on match day and the pub car park is deserted. Where can they be? At twenty-five past – still nobody. At half-past, thirteen of the lads lurch out of the public bar led by the captain of the day.

'There you are. Bit small for a prop aren't you? Still, it is best you play there. None of us has had any experience of prop-ing, you see.'

'Well, er, actually – neither have I.'

No sooner had he stopped talking than the No. 3 jersey came over the roof of the Mini and a prop it was. The changing-room is a converted garage – for converted read a row of twelve six-inch nails, spaced out and banged along one wall to act as hooks and an old-fashioned

GENTLY!
HE'S A BIT SMALL
FOR A PROP!
The NAGS HEAD
THUD!

handbasin with a copper cold-water tap hung over it which, detached from the wall, bangs loudly every time a car passes. The ritual of borrowing boots and bits of tape and vaseline is over quickly as no one has much of anything, including boots. So, with half-backs kitted out in smooth-soled gym-shoes and one man short, into the car park we go where two Minis and a tandem wait to carry fourteen of us to the ground three miles away. The realization that everyone in his car has heavily vaselined thighs does not do much for the marriage prospects of the driver hoping to take his young lady out in her nice new dress that night.

On to the ground where the visitors have been waiting, changed, for some thirty-five minutes after deciding to put their kit on in their own bus because no-one told them which pub we use for changing.

Now a real problem: there are no posts at one end. Also, the pitch markings have faded into the overgrown pastureland which still has sheep grazing between the half-way line and the twenty-five. The two lads on the tandem arrive late and are immediately sent back to steal the flagpoles from outside the pub for use as goalposts. The captain talks to their bus driver who consents to referee provided play is limited to just one half or ten minutes each way.

During the game four players develop a serious skin complaint caused by constantly falling into the droppings of various species of livestock which occasionally stroll back onto the field of play; one of them collides with our winger in full flight causing him a near-fatal injury and a certain month's confinement in the local infirmary. Back in the changing-room afterwards, the fight to get a leg under the only tap is as hard a physical test as the game itself. Anyone who did remember to bring a towel finds it already used by the winner of the race to the tap. The final insult is the captain asking for a large match fee and a donation to the kitty so that we can buy them a pint and a pork pie in the pub.

Consider the contrast when you arrive at your first senior match to find a match programme with a profile on you. They give you a shirt, some socks, all neatly laid out, and there's a 'No Smoking' sign over the dressing-room door. A track-suited masseur asks: 'Got any pet muscles, son?' The coach has given his deadly serious team talk. You run onto the pitch to be applauded by a huge crowd gathered to see you and your colleagues perform well-rehearsed moves to perfection. The front row of the grandstand is full of typewriters and telephones relaying to the waiting world details of your every move. The game over and a sit-down dinner in the players' lounge. The jugs of free beer flow, and loitering journalists trouble you with questions about your availability for this year's international matches. The heady heights of the fashionable club are enjoyed by everyone lucky enough to get to that level. But there comes a time when the legs lose their zip and the mind is dulled by the depredations of one-armed bandits, women and the night-life. At that time the small club beckons once again: 'Come and put something back into the club that made you.'

THE REFEREE

The only man in this chapter with his own profile. We put him here not maliciously – to emphasize what a complete outsider he is – but because he simply didn't fit in anywhere else. He is, after all, the man who does the job that no-one else wants to do. Referees are blamed for all manner of things from the state of the pitch to the weather and even accused of downright cheating. They arrive for the game alone and stand around afterwards hoping someone will speak to them.

If the home team lose and have what they consider to be a raw deal from him it can be difficult for the referee to get a shower when he is sharing a dressing-room with them. They are likely to make him feel about as welcome as a fart in a space suit. In the bar someone who has reffed once or twice and knows the predicament he is in will walk over and share some small talk with him. And as the evening goes on one of the team will forget what a diabolical cheat he has been and offer him a beer out of their jug. This can be construed by the ref as a sign of acceptance. If he is offered a drink out of the jug of the losers then he knows that he's had a good game.

Referees give their services for free and by and large fall into the category of unsuccessful players who are still doing their bit for the game. There is however a dangerous animal lurking in referee's clothing. He is the ambitious I'm-going-somewhere referee. He sees himself as the most important man on the field. A famous old referee once wrote that 'a referee's aim on the field should be to be No. 31 not No. 1.' Many of today's up-and-coming referees do not subscribe to this view. Ask yourself what sort of creature could arrive at a game with three different-coloured jerseys carefully pressed and folded, two pairs of shorts (one black, one white), two notepads, three pencils, two watches, two whistles and a handkerchief.

After safely selecting the day's kit he will strut out onto the field, his hair perfectly in place to be marked by some anonymous adjudicator on his appearance before he ever puts the whistle to his lips. Do not trust this man especially if you are a regular biff-bang forward out to enjoy your Saturday afternoon run-in with an old sparring partner, for he is bound to ruin your fun. When he is issuing you with a warning he will

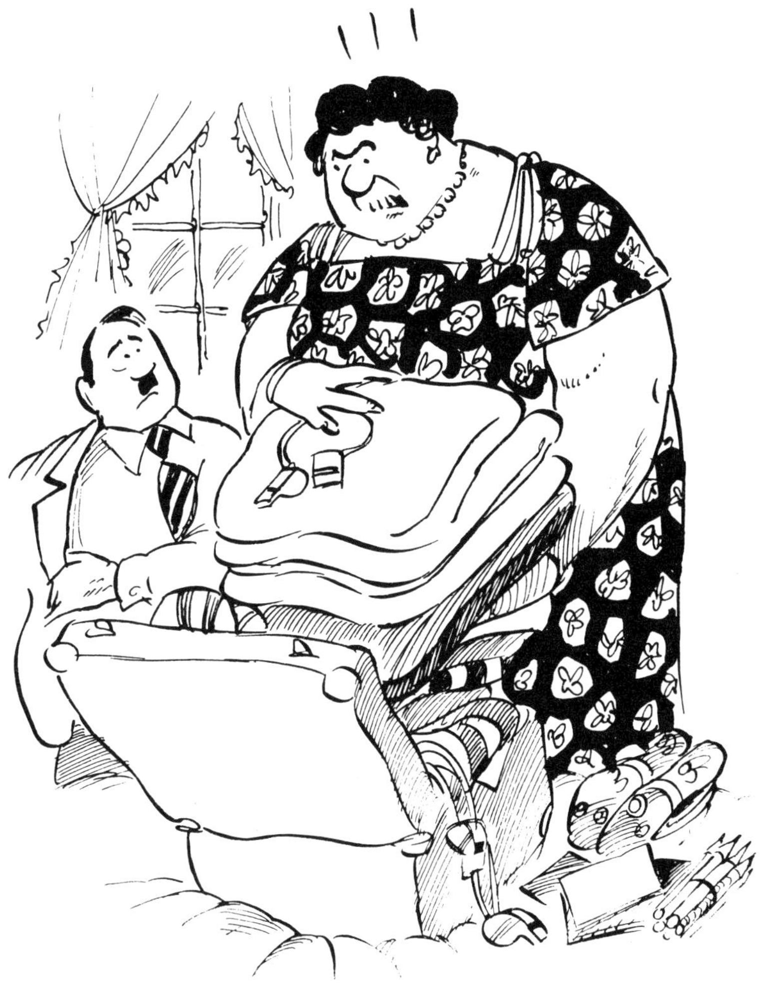

HERE'S YOUR KIT... AND IF YOU LOSE CONTROL OF THE GAME YOU'VE GOT **ME** TO ANSWER TO!

walk ten yards back and call you towards him. He will gesticulate with his finger in an attempt to belittle you and at the same time serve notice to all those watching, including the adjudicator, that he is going to stand no nonsense from you and what a good ref he is. He always blows the whistle at the first ruck, line-out or scrum, not because anything is amiss but to Stamp His Authority on the game.

The ambitious referee spends his life aiming to get on this or that panel. He prides himself on the fact that he is conscientious enough to stay in the bar hours after each game to chat things over with players or committees alike. This is all part of the con-man that he is. For if you find something that he missed he will come out with some crap about being unsighted or baffle you with a recent change in the law. He is never wrong or will never admit it. The top refs are always very intelligent men, just look at the jobs they do: teachers, lecturers, senior policmen, dentists, doctors, solicitors, headmasters, senior sales executives, high ranking military officers – there aren't many plumbers or bricklayers on the international panel of any country.

Most referees at some time or other will earn a degree of notoriety be sending someone off the field in disgrace. Having sent the lad from the field, these highly intelligent individuals will try to justify their action by worsening the details of the case in a written report. Then they sit back and wait to hear how many months their victim has been suspended for. This will make a lovely talking point at the monthly referees' meeting when they all gather to discuss more ways to spoil our Saturday afternoons. Their greatest ambition is to referee a television match, take a video recording of it and play it until they die or become adjudicators.

THE TOUR

The rugby tour is an integral part of each season, whether it is the end-of-season long-weekend beer-up with one match or a major overseas tour with four games. The well-established tradition of door-breaking, trophy collecting and beer-drinking competitions is frowned upon by the senior club administrators and considered much worse than anything they got up to. The tour tales get bigger and better every time they are told. The effect on the youngster making his first tour is to try and do everything he heard so-and-so did last year only from a greater height, distance, or in a shorter time.

The first half-dozen to put their names up on the notice board, for some reason, never get to go. This may have something to do with the ten per cent down-payment asked for when indicating one's intention to confirm. The other twenty-nine do go but never pay the deposit anyway let alone the amounts due for hotel, beer kitty and travel. The tour organizer who is often the club secretary cannot go himself because he is quite ill from the strain of collecting the money and finally he has to subsidize the open-side from his own pocket.

Most tours start on a Friday. This is to ensure the team a good night's sleep before the tour's opening match and so, having actually got them all to the hotel, checked in and had dinner, the alickadoos, team manager and coach go off to the opposition's clubhouse for a quiet eve-of-match drink, leaving the completely trustworthy and responsible players to finish off their glasses of orange juice before going to their beds. At this point things go slightly off-course. The No. 8 is deep in conversation with a most attractive young lady and two of her not-so-attractive friends. The open-side is into his fifth pint and is trying to get a sing-song going. The captain (Corgi) is being chatted up by a queer sailor and the outside-half is desperately trying to find the hooker with a view to approaching the two spare ugly birds with the No. 8.

The alickadoos return to the team's hotel just before 2 am, not paralytically drunk but definitely the worse for wear. They slip quietly into the bar for a nightcap and are met with the uproarious laughter and singing of the playing strength. Ashen-faced and trying to disguise his own unsteady gait, the trainer confronts Corgi.

'What's this?'

The diminutive half-back attempts a reply but his mouth just hangs open. The trainer goes on: 'Can no-one be trusted? All the work we've done and now look at you.'

Sweat begins to drop from his forehead over his glass eye, giving the impression of tear drops. The team hard man puts his arm around the grieving trainer. 'Come on, Cyclops. Don't get all upset and mess the tour up. We won't let you down tomorrow.'

Cyclops is not impressed. 'I'm going up. Team meeting in the morning, the coach's room, 11am. Be there.'

The morning comes around too early for most. Corgi looks at his watch. 10.59am. 'Christ, where's my clothes?' He opens every cupboard door and pulls half the drawers out before realizing he has slept fully clothed, shoes as well. His room-mate, the hooker, has obviously not slept in his bed. He finds the coach's room in one minute flat and walks defiantly in to find the room full. He is last in and the only one to have missed breakfast.

'Sorry lads, forgot the room number.'

The team talk confirms his worst fears. The coach has decided to play a fast open game since it is a lovely summer day, the conditions perfect for throwing the ball around. On the bus, en route to the ground, the open-side sits quietly, not at all sure he can hold on to his breakfast. Once there, he suggests we ask for fifteen minutes each way. The dressing-room is alive with the No. 8's name. Rumour has

HREE PINTS OF SPECIAL AND
WHAT ARE THE LADIES
HAVING?

spread that he screwed all three of them last night whilst the hooker and the outside-half watched. 'Groper' is wide-eyed and in fantasy land again.

'Did he do them all at once, or one at a time?' he asks the hooker.

'Don't be so bloody stupid. Of course he did them one at a time.'

'What about me? I didn't get any.'

The coach chimes in: 'OK, lads. Four minutes to go. You had a good night last night. Now you know what we are here for. This lot think we are a bunch of hicks up from the country. Let's show them. Groper, they won the toss so we kick off. Hit their big bloke straight away. If he gets up our heavy artillery will be right behind you so don't worry about retaliation.'

From the kick-off our plans go disastrously wrong. They gather unchallenged, and spin it along the back line to score without a hand being laid on any of them. There is worse to come. Having heard about our antics the night before, they are running everything from anywhere to everywhere. Ten points, seventeen points, twenty points, 32 – 0 and forty minutes still to play. Both our centres are complaining about hamstring trouble, the hard man has lost two teeth and the referee has discovered his sister was deflowered by our winger the night before. The scrum bangs together, the tight-head chuckles to the lock: 'Hey, did you hear that? Dobbin and his sister!' The open-side, green with envy: 'Yer, the crafty little bastard. He kept that quiet didn't he?'

The débâcle over, it's into the clubhouse. Now the tour starts in earnest. All the silly bar games are in operation to get everyone past it in the shortest possible time. Left-handed drinking, no smoking, no talking to committee men. All transgressions are punished by a pint straight down, served from a dirty enamel jug held by the captain.

Sunday morning and court is called. These sessions have now become an essential part of tours. They are a good way of getting everyone together as well as disciplining certain players who have broken the laws of team conduct; penalties are to drink excessive amounts of alcohol and pay small fines with which to buy more of the stuff thereby setting a perpetual drink-buying system in motion. Without exception the charges are trumped up. Any defence offered usually means a heavier punishment. No-one is ever found not guilty.

The judge is Groper and Bumper is the prosecuting council.

The first charge is against the open-side for lowering the standard of the team by having sexual intercourse with a dead whore in the blind-side's bed in the early hours of the morning. Chief prosecution witness is the blind-side himself. The accused enters a plea of guilty but with mitigating circumstances. In evidence he admits having committed the act but maintains she was drunk and not dead at the time he actually got across her. The blind-side under cross-examination confirms going back to his room and finding the accused in a compromising position and that in his view rigor mortis had set in some hours before. Groper stops the case there and then, and puts on the black cap:

'This has been one of the most disgusting cases it has been my misfortune to hear and I find it impossible to consider any plea for leniency. You will drink one pint of depth-charge, which will consist of one pint of beer, one measure of gin, one measure of brandy, one measure of whisky. Straight down without a pause and pay one pound into the beer kitty.'

The boys nod agreement and then break into open laughter and hand-clapping as the No. 8 is charged with sexual greed, and non-consideration of a team-mate. They have been dying to find out the explicit details of Friday night's encounter. The outside-half cannot wait to get his own back by recounting the story.

'Me and the hooker had bought drinks for the two uglies and left Snake to deal with the very attractive friend for a full two hours before disturbing him with a request for second use of the bed.'

The evidence given was damning. The No. 8 was reported quite purposely to have given the two uglies a glimpse of his now-famous weapon while putting on his trousers, at which both ladies were overcome with lust and dived on him. The No. 8, with some justification, felt the greed was on their part, but his defence was found by the judge to be unacceptable.

'To make your team-mates watch this act of lust really was the most reprehensible thing to do. However I have heard via the grape-vine that because of your outstanding performance with all three of these women

THE USUAL, LADIES... TWO DE CHARGES?

that night our team has been nominated for the BBC Team of the Year Award and in view of this you will drink two pints of ordinary beer straight down instead of three which this thoroughly distasteful episode warrants and you are excused paying any fine at all.'

The following day sees a lull in alcoholic activity whilst the team begin to build up to the second game and a chance to salvage something from the ruins of last Saturday's performance. Most touring sides manage to win one game and so can go home to tell tales of poor refereeing and bad luck in the opening game and scintillating performances in the subsequent matches. The team's kleptomaniacs, having left home with a toothbrush in the top pocket and an empty suitcase, return with a battery of road signs, cutlery and assorted bar-room furniture. The heavy artillery man has a badly bruised arm and the team secretary is contacting the teams we played against in a bid to find the owner.

THE SEVENS

Sevens are an original form of torture for those playing but offer a lazy afternoon in the beer tent for the spectators. The annual competition is played at the tail-end of each season and brings with it the problem of selecting seven athletes and a replacement. Most clubs do not have seven athletes let alone a replacement. The hunt is on for fast-running, hard-tackling individuals who are available on a Sunday afternoon, or the nearest thing to them. In accordance with the democratic policies followed by most clubs the availability sheet is pinned to the notice board with date and details some two weeks before the event is staged. This will allow several practice sessions in the specialist art of sevens to be held before the big day. None of first-team's backs is available but every forward from the first, second and third teams is willing to give it a go. The team, when announced, brings gasps of horror and is listed as follows:

Loose-head prop

Is a Colts No. 8. He stands 6ft 6in, weighs 10 stone, is wet through and is chosen because he can double as a line-out forward. He spent last summer perfecting his jumping technique by feeding the giraffes at the local zoo.

PUT IT IN STRAIGHT, DAMMIT!
ZOO

Hooker
Is the third-team hooker, aged 22, who after four years with the club has yet to win a tight-head duel with anyone but can run like a rabbit and is a world-class thrower-in.

Tight-head prop
The second-team full-back moved up just for the sevens because he is a bit overweight but is a recognized goal-kicker and has a more than useful head-butt. For some time now he has been trying to cultivate a cauliflower ear; he has won no other trophies in rugby and feels it would be something for him to show his grandchildren.

Scrum-half
Is the first-team scrum-half and captain, Corgi. Determined not to let the club image suffer due to non-availablity of first-team players.

Outside-half
A Fijian basketball international here doing a medical course, who has recently been playing centre for our 4th XV. He is a one-handed passer and a two-footed tackler. His party-piece is to eat the hottest Indian curry and rice with his fingers.

Centre
The centre is a recently demobbed military policeman who played for us before joining up and is hoping to re-establish himself as a hard-tackling, non-passing, ball-dropping centre.

The Wing
A speedy South African Provincial player who is over here on his holidays and was pulled in to make up the team at the last minute. He would have won the Man of the Competition Award if he had been in a team good enough to give him a pass.

The result – knocked out in the first match, but only 14 – 0 and as we don't have to play any more games we certainly can't be disgraced going down by an astronomical score to a team of college boys containing seven even-timers who have been practising all year for this one event. Our performance is nevertheless considered so bad that the host club refuse to give us any tea tickets and have threatened to break off fixtures at all levels. Matters are made worse when three of our 1st XV backs are seen warming up with an All Star invitation seven, having had a bye in the first round. The club's senior alickadoos call an emergency meeting between the temporary toilets and the beer tent.

'Why weren't those three available for us?'

All eyes focus on the poor old secretary. 'They didn't put their names on the board'. The meeting ends with the words 'full internal inquiry' issuing from the lips of the president who is in his element when there is any shit flying. By the time the competition ends most of the team and committee are well-oiled enough to allow the three players who represented the All Star team instead of us – and, incidentally, won the whole bloody competition – to ride home on the team bus, telling us how easy it all was and how they wished they had known we had entered a team.

ALICKADOOS AND HANGERS-ON

club is not a club without its ragged battalion of non-playing camp-followers. In general, their nuisance value varies in proportion to the size of their mouths – which puts the Rugby Heavy at the top of that list, although certain Media Men run them pretty close. But let's begin with some of the (mainly) good guys.

CLUB COMMITTEE MEN

Basically a bunch of sound blokes who years ago had been the lads themselves. Their favourite conversation-piece is their playing days. They love to meet players of their own vintage from other clubs and reminisce. They give their services free and are hurt when today's players call them alickadoos or similar names since each still sees himself as one of the lads. There is always some deadwood on the committee. Usually they are the men who never played the game but are so often at the clubhouse bar that they almost fall into the job. They never do as much as sell a raffle ticket but are always first to put their name up for the tour. When their turn comes around for bar duty they are always ill or doing overtime. But we mustn't tar all committee men with the same brush. Without sound committees our clubs, the backbone of the game, would be in a sorry state.

NATIONAL COMMITTEE MEN

The first ingredient needed to become a committee man of a national rugby union is to know absolutely bugger-all about rugby or the people who play it. The second is to drink gin and tonic in large measures. The third is to be a high-flying veterinary surgeon, an air-commodore, a lieutenant-colonel, a rear-admiral or at the very least a successful businessman. If you have been to Oxford or Cambridge it will help. If you have trained once with the Harlequins you are a certainty. Others arrive at the top via the Mothercare 3rd XV.

The individuals that serve on these committees must be on an ego trip, otherwise they would have been happy to serve on their own club committees. Almost without exception they are aiming for higher things, and the higher they get the nearer the presidency comes. They always deny with some vehemence that this is why they do it but they give the best international match tickets away to business connections who have nothing to do with rugby in order to boost their own commercial standing. They never miss a free dinner. Those with double-barrelled names are streets in front of the others in the race for the presidency.

THE PRESIDENT

A figurehead who does pathetically little that is any use to anyone. He is between sixty and 105 and has spent his life working towards the presidency. At club level the only way to lose the job is to die or rape the treasurer's wife. Higher up the scale at national or provincial level the president is appointed for one year only, after creep-arsing his way through umpteen committees and the vice-presidency. He then swears that this will be the year that something gets done. Nothing changes. His moment of glory is to be in the team photograph. He will sit in the front row wearing a sheepskin coat, next to the man who is holding the ball, and smile. After this he will go off to the grandstand with his hip flask and his rug to get quietly pissed while the boys get on with the job. He sees himself as the most important person in rugby, and has designed a strapless scrum-cap. Once bet his balls to a bag of sweets that his son – the club right-centre – would finish two games in succession. Is now soprano in a male-voice choir.

ENUINE 100% WOOL
McCREEPARSE TARTAN

TREASURER

A pillar of society. Is a bank manager or accountant or at the very least a building-society employee. The sort of bloke who has bowls of fruit and nuts around the house when it's not Christmas. Noted for his annual appeal for prompt payment of subs and match fees. No-one takes seriously what he says about the situation facing the club ('If we are not careful...'). He regrets that we cannot have floodlights or our clubhouse extension during the next twelve months unless there is a sharp increase in bar takings. The meeting ends and he doesn't speak again for twelve months. Six months later work begins on the bar extension and the floodlights. Was a hooker in his playing days but retired after losing four against the head to a scrummaging machine.

CLUB SECRETARY

The backbone of the club, has to keep everyone happy. All the non-playing members are after him for international match tickets, and all the players ask him to sign their expense forms before giving them to the treasurer. He sorts out every little detail from marking out the pitch when the groundsman is ill to shaking hands with the Lord Mayor when the clubhouse is opened. He has to contend with reams of bullshit from the Rugby Union. In years gone by he rode a bike and wore a flat cap and bicycle clips. Today he drives a family car or a Honda motorbike. If he is secretary of a gate-taking club he has two cars and two Hondas. He spends his life on the phone dealing with late cry-offs from injured players and insurance claims from those who were injured last year. He swears he won't do it for another year but he will weaken when the president offers gracious thanks at the AGM. He loves the lads to talk rugby with him. It brings out the Walter Mitty in him and after three pints he should have played for the World. Never talks about his playing days to anyone who is old enough to have seen him play.

FIXTURES SECRETARY

A down-to-earth honest individual who usually works in a large office using the firm's phone to improve the quality of his club's fixtures while at the same time fending off what he considers to be less important clubs who are trying to improve their own status. With the advent of league competitions he may soon become confined to running around the fixture exchanges trying to fix up games after we have been knocked out of the cup and the league programme is completed.

The fixtures secretary is almost unknown to the players. He quietly puffs his pipe or sips his half standing at the end of the bar quite anonymously. But heaven help him if he ever makes a cock-up, like sending the lads to a game that doesn't exist or getting us there at 12 o'clock for an evening kick-off, or having two teams arrive on Saturday when we have only one to play against them. It's all too easy to get it wrong. He works years in advance having to make fixtures for four or five teams. He also has the unpleasant task of telephoning a club and telling them that one of our players is getting married and we can't play today, and the equally unpleasant task of rushing round trying to fix a game for the boys when some other team have called off for similar reasons. The fixtures secretary has no interest in higher office in the club and is quite happy to do his job to the best of his ability. He does, however, have a sneaking ambition to get onto the selection committee. He was a useful prop in his prime, but called it a day when they asked him to run between scrums.

BAR STEWARD

The most wealthy man in the club. Can be seen at the local cash-and-carry buying his own bottles of spirits for sale over the bar. Has a job separating his own profit from the club's at the end of an evening. Never goes on holiday in case someone else empties the fruit machines. Always keeps the bar open for a late one except when we are playing a police team. He makes a fortune on sandwiches cut by his wife and loves to walk around the club with a bunch of keys in his hand as an outward sign of his authority. He appears upset if the team loses and happy if they win. He really doesn't give a damn as long as he's paid. Club stewards

have a high turnover rate. None of them lasts long. It's better for the lads themselves to run the bar on a rota system.

THE GROUNDSMAN

A harmless soul who seeks nothing for himself. Can be seen on training nights pumping up balls, cleaning down corner-flag poles. On Saturday he will mark out five pitches without complaint and paint goal posts all Sunday afternoon. His pleasure is to hear a compliment about his playing surface. On his half-days and during the summer months he will mow and sow the fields with loving care. He is also responsible for keeping the baths and showers clean. He has two halves after each match and doesn't really care if the team win or lose, as long as the field is OK. He has never attended the annual dinner and is worth his weight in gold.

THE GATEMAN, PROGRAMME SELLERS AND CAR PARK ATTENDANT

These are some of the most powerful men in rugby. They decide whether you get into the patrons' tarmacadamed car park next to the lounge bar or the field behind a pub two miles away.

Gatemen fall into two categories. First is the professional gateman employed from week to week by the clubs large enough to get a decent crowd at home games. Usually a pensioner with an old but tidy gaberdene mac and trilby hat. His wages are minimal but like the commissionaire at a grand hotel he lives on tips. The gateman is a wizard with even the most up-to-date computerized turnstiles and lives off the money paid by people thin enough to slip through the turnstile without turning the counter. These gatemen cannot afford to miss a Saturday even when dying of pneumonia in case the gate-takings go up and the administrators realize they have been cooking the books.

The second type is the temporary gateman employed at clubs not used to staging big games. He is always in evidence when a small club gets to the later stages of a cup competition or when a major touring club plays on a club ground. He wears a duffel coat with a yellow arm-band marked 'Steward' and lets all his mates in for free and keeps as much of the money collected on the gate as possible for the boys' drink kitty afterwards. On the Monday following the game he calls for an internal inquiry as the club has failed to make as much money as had been anticipated out of such a great day.

At all major matches tickets are sold in advance and the gateman's job suddenly becomes very unpopular. There is a rush on to become programme-sellers and car-park attendants. They are lucrative positions. The car-park attendant takes your money, points you 'Over there' and conveniently forgets to give you a numbered ticket receipt which means one less to be accounted for. The programme-sellers have a much more sophisticated deal, taking two packs of fifty programmes, sprinting off into the crowd and paying for one pack thirty minutes later. This is neatly judged to happen two minutes after the kick-off when the noise and the excitement of 94 such programme-sellers paying in at the same time serves to confuse the programme distributor, himself an old-age pensioner who does the job twice a year and is furious that he was allocated the task of distributing and is unable to take his cut of the bounty.

TWICKERS, DOCTOR!

THE RUGBY HEAVY

Lists among his cultural interests beer, curry and chips, ballroom dancing and Coronation Street. He will always be a member of a major club. In this way he has a chance to hobnob with the leading players of the day. He will always be at the big games and internationals. As soon as his hero is within ten yards of the ball he will tell, for all to hear, how he had a

beer with him last week. It is his habit to badger any player of any standing into a conversation of some sort after buying the beer and hoping the great man himself will say a few words to him – or even buy him a beer in return.

A heavy is easily spotted, he will be wearing a blazer with a large pocket badge and both lapels covered in various rugby pins. His tie will be symbolic in some way – a triple crown, a Springbok head or a New Zealand fern. If he decides to go out in a sweater he will wear the same symbolic tie hanging ridiculously outside his sweater and on his chest will be some equally symbolic badge for all to admire. He always drinks pints. He can answer any question on rugby and has never been seen looking at another woman, never mind talking to one. Even so he frequently gets the rolling-pin treatment from the wife for coming home late, pissed and under suspicion of womanizing. The wife need not have worried: he had only been down at the club looking at internationals and arguing about everything from that day's game to who should or should not be in the national side. His life's ambition is to get an international match ball signed by the boys and then show it around telling everyone that he knows them all personally. He talks a great game and during his playing days was automatic choice as fifth-team touch-judge.

THE RUGBY SUPPORTER

Different from the rugby heavy in that he is prepared to watch rugby, have a few pints in the local and go home to face the wife before daybreak. Can be divided into two types. The first of these will travel on an official supporters' coach, two barrels of beer between them, the emergency door open for an emergency pee and a ton of sandwiches somewhere in the middle. Some arrive at the game without tickets and those who do have tickets stand in the rain sharing wet sandwiches with the man behind them. They are the backbone of the game and they don't give a toss about the best seats as long as they see the game and their team win. They leave home together but arrive home in ones or twos anytime between Sunday and the following Wednesday. The story of the weekend will be told for months afterwards and they will all be there on their home ground the following weekend faithfully following their club heroes.

The second type of supporter will see maybe one or two games a year and will only watch internationals. He will sit in the best seats and will have enjoyed elevenses followed by a sumptuous lunch with champagne before taking his place in the stand. He gets his tickets from business connections and sits with a rug over his knees talking regular swigs from a solid silver hip-flask. He doesn't mind who wins as long as everyone has a jolly nice day.

THE BUS DRIVER

He is an integral part of the team and very often doubles as third-team sponge man. He will wait from early evening when the game ends until the early hours of the morning when the outside-half reappears from behind the clubhouse with some grateful young lady. On the bus and heading home he will listen intently to the outside-half explaining to the lads how he did it. He knows the lads are hungry and will drive around strange towns and back alleys until he finds a Chinese take-away. He will drive home with the residue of the special fried rice dripping down the back of his neck from a perfect offspin delivery by the replacement prop standing by the emergency door. He will stop within seconds of a shout for the lads to take a piss. He has the thankless task of cleaning down the bus after a weekend away with the fourth and fifth teams, which brings him a haul of one bucket of spew, five used contraceptives, four girlie magazines, twelve half-eaten packets of chips, various empty foil food containers, and numberless empty beer cans and bottles. He disposes of them all without complaint. He never gets invited to the annual dinner.

RUGBY MEDIA MEN

The rugby media man almost always starts as the local rag reporter and is known affectionately as 'Scoop' to the lads. He never writes anything really nasty about any player even when a diabolical performance thoroughly warrants it. He drinks after the match with anyone who will feed him juicy stories about anything that is not so controversial that he

U.F.C. ANNUAL DINNER
SHOULD'VE INVITED THE BUS DRIVER.. HE'D HAVE LIKED THIS!

won't be able to drink in the club next week. Only later, when climbing the rugby ladder of success onto a national newspaper, does he become a danger to all.

He will delve into all sorts of detail in an attempt to find an angle on a player. Very often the angle has nothing at all to do with the individual's playing ability. This is especially true of writers employed by the popular Press. A writer touring another country with a national, provincial or senior club team will busy himself talking to players and building contacts until he finds himself sufficiently well in to ask the player what he did in a game or what he thought of it. He can then write a passable piece of copy giving the impression to his readers that he has some idea of what is actually going on. In fact few of them know anything that they are not told by the lads themselves and often need to use TV rerun facilities to confirm what they think they might have seen.

Writers, or correspondents as they are called on the posh papers, are never to be trusted. With a stroke of the pen these fibre-tipped assassins can ruin the career of some promising young man or break the heart of a genuine club player who was only doing his best and knows he will never play for the World. And yet these highly paid professional observers are never called upon actually to get out there and do the job themselves. (Listen to their howls of protest – highly paid indeed!) Perhaps before they complain about the pittance they earn they should consider that it is a bloody sight more than most the players they criticize are ever likely to get.

With TV coverage Rugby Union has become a much-followed international sport and it is only sensible with the eye of the world upon it that it should be presented in a competent and proper way by hand-picked professionals with a thorough knowledge of the laws and an understanding of the part each player is required to play as well as the domestic details like whose wife had a bouncing baby boy this week, who has changed jobs from teacher to sports representative since being selected for the national team.

Different countries have different styles of covering the big day. In South Africa, for example, TV was late arriving and commentators are not yet used to working from TV monitors. Their only experience has been on radio. The result is an unnecessarily fast commentary delivering so much detail you would think the audience could not see the screen. Fortunately what they do say is fair, unbiased and informed comment. Unfortunately it loses some of its impact because of its similarity to a high-revving motorbike passing close to the front door on a quiet Sunday morning. Another problem for watchers of big-time rugby on television in South Africa is that the camera occasionally misses the point of the action and wanders off into the crowd for a general view at the same time as the greatest athlete in the republic is in full flight for the line. Just to confuse the issue, at half-time the commentary changes from English to Afrikaans or vice-versa. The very fact that TV cameras are there means you are watching the best international players whose every move is being watched by young children, mothers, grandparents, and is of national importance.

In New Zealand this also applies, but the commentators have a great taste for realism and would not think of turning a blind eye to the odd left hook. Quite the contrary. 'And that's a beaut left hook in there from Smith. Trouble's been brewing up for some time now. But Jones is back in there immediately with a hard kick straight in the lower abdomen'. The general style of commentary in New Zealand tends to be as fair and unbiased as they think media men in other parts of the world are. By and large it works. But it is not too difficult to tell the difference between the calm practical voice complimenting the opposition on a 'fine try' and the shrill speedy patter building up to a crescendo of screams as the All-Blacks clinch the series with a corner-flag try after a thirty-yard run leaving six defenders sprawling. There is nevertheless something to be said for the honesty of commentaries in New Zealand because by including the odd bout of fisticuffs in the commentary they are openly telling us what is actually happening. Some observers may of course interpret the relish with which the commentator tells it as a sign of his condoning villainy.

During commentaries in the UK the opposite position is taken by commentators. They stand firmly in the Establishment's camp and talk as if they were not there to comment on the match but to protect the image of Rugby Union if it's the last thing they do. 'My wurrd, it's warming up in there and the referee's having a word with John Bullen. Well Mr Pitcombe is a very experienced referee. He'll stand no nonsense from this burrrly forward. You can see he's a big fellow, weighs around 17 stones, farms in the shadow of the Severn Bridge when he's not training for rugby. And Mr Pitcombe has awarded a penalty-kick. Rightly so, there is no place in rugby for that sort of skullduggery.' All this and the commentator never actually saw anything happen but is prepared to back the man in the middle blind, or, in refereeing terms, 'unsighted'.

Now consider the radio commentator stuck up on the roof of the grandstand being showered in birdshit and unable to stop talking because he has no visual means of contact between himself and his audience. It is undoubtedly true that as we cannot see him or the game he is talking about he can tell us anything he likes: provided he gets the scorers and the sequence correct, and the actual result at the end is right, he has a job for life. We know he tries his best to reflect the ebb and flow of the game and to suggest that he has given us eighty minutes' pure crap would be quite wrong. It has to be admitted, however, that there is much more scope for the radio commentator to make mistakes and get away with it than his TV counterpart who is watching the same game as his viewers. Without exception radio commentators are dying to get a break in television and most of them write for one or two newspapers as well as doing bits for radio. If the commentator himself does not aspire to these heights then he has an assistant who certainly does.

THE CLUB DOCTOR, RUB-A-DUB MAN OR MEDICAL OFFICER

Many clubs not fortunate enough to have a proper doctor in the playing ranks or on the committee, and who recognize the importance of having someone who knows something about the human body, will appoint a medical officer. These officers could be St John's Ambulance Certificate holders (Part I, failed), veterinary surgeons, or someone whose sole job is to drive the victim to the nearest hospital as quickly as possible and get him back for the piss-up or the coach home.

Medical officers have varying effects on players. The sight of a sheepskin-coated GP lurching unsteadily out of the bar and across the field has seen many a hitherto unconscious player jump to his feet shouting: 'I'm OK, I'm OK'. The gravity of a facial cut fades into insignificance when faced with a vet trying his first stitching job on a human or the rub-a-dub man sharpening up a knitting needle and calling for cotton.

The last major injury the club had is still talked about. The day the club cripple became the club cripple. He was suddenly seen lying flat out after being involved in the only ruck that he'd been near all that year. He had obviously broken his leg. Both teams realized the seriousness of the situation and immediately signalled for a stretcher which was carried out by the GP who had been drinking heavily since midday, the vet, the ex-St John's Ambulance man and a bystander who said he knew all about this kind of thing because he had broken his leg during World War I. Then with the full permission of the other three this old war hero began to massage the fracture vigorously saying 'At least this will keep the circulation going' and trying to cheer our man up with 'It's not too much to worry about – if you were a horse they would have shot you'. The players began to get cold. After 20 minutes it was discovered that no-one had actually telephoned for the ambulance and to save wasting any more time our hospital transport man bundled the injured man onto the back of his 500-cc Honda and began the hair-raising and arse-aching ride to hospital. Because he got lost several times on the way to the hospital the victim finally arrived there two hours after the incident and just in time for the surgeon to amputate because acute gangrene had set in. Still, the club stood by him. They organized a collection for him and so he did not feel out of things gave him a job as the club fund-raising chairman, which turned out to be a good move because he's a much better fund-raiser than he ever was a player.

THE SELECTORS

These are the unsung heroes of world rugby. They give their time for nothing and get absolutely no thanks from anyone. Their wives complain they are always either watching a match or at a selection meeting. The players think they are all crazy and know nothing about anything. The Press criticize the selectors of a losing team but never praise those of a winning team. Of course there are some plusses. The players at least do know who they are and do like to rub shoulders. Provincial and national selectors are usually made most welcome and indeed can expect red-carpet treatment from a club hoping that one of their boys might get a favourable report. This doesn't of course mean that a selector knows any more about the game than the groundsman but simply that he is a vehicle on which someone can ride to a higher rung on the rugby ladder. If he visits the same club twelve months after he has come off the national selection committee there will certainly be a difference in his reception. The national or provincial selector gets all sorts of anonymous calls and letters telling him whom to pick and whom not to pick. He has to put up with a player's mum sitting behind him in the grandstand, constantly referring to her son by his surname or number so as to bring her little lad to his attention. Selectors have such a hard time from everyone it's a wonder they do it – it must be for the glory and the power of being a big shot. It is a well-known fact that certain selectors have a limited if not total lack of knowledge of the game.

Most clubs have their selection meeting on the first training night of the week. The ideal number of selectors is nine. One will be the coach who always thinks he knows more than the others and is also close enough to the players to argue certain points on their behalf. Like more money for the beer kitty and two days longer on tour this year. The chairman was a first-class player who pals up with the coach at most social functions in the hope people will think he knows as much as the coach. The chairman will also make all public announcements and do all the dirty jobs like telling a player the reason why he's been dropped. The captains of the first, second and third teams are automatically on selection and attend occasionally. The other four consist, firstly, of two extrovert touch-judges – neither of whom has played the game at any time in his life, for reasons ranging from near-fatal accidents carrying out the corner-flags to alcoholic poisoning; they have major says in who does and who doesn't play. The other two are senior and loyal club administrators who between them have held office for something like the last four decades and who are angling for life-membership. They have little or no say in selection and always take the blame when things are going badly.

International selection committees are very similar in their make-up to club panels except that some members have played at a higher level and are therefore considered to be well-versed in the rigours of international rugby. Seven is the number of selectors usually appointed to choose the nation's best XV and although they are selecting players for the international game, three of the seven will not have had international experience. On the other hand they may have written a couple of books on the theory of refereeing, weight-lifting or grandstand building. The chairman will have graduated from or be lecturing at some university or other and the coach will be a recently retired international, whose claim to fame is his after-match rendition of a tribal war-dance learnt on tour in South Africa. The last two are tight forwards considered hard by Harlequin standards and brought in to select a few villains that will cause the opposition just enough bother not to get the selectors sacked for inciting violence.

YES...THE SOUND OF KNITTING NEEDLES IS REALLY PUTTING HIM OFF HIS STROKE!
DO NOT DISTUR

THE WIFE, MISTRESS OR GIRL-FRIEND

The woman has played an increasing role in rugby club life in recent years. Indeed it was not so long ago that a woman in the clubhouse was unheard of. Now they not only do the teas but they run their own social events and attend the annual dinner, which has become a dinner-dance, and have the nerve to suggest that speeches should not be too long this year so that there can be more time for dancing. They are even making their way onto tours and organizing their own trips to some hot spot where the old man can't get a blow-by-blow account of their weekend.

Tea ladies were formerly the wives of committee men or players, but nowadays we see a new breed of tea lady or clubhouse lady. Young, single, with an eye for a particular individual and permanency, they often nail him and force him into retirement, neither of them to be seen in the clubhouse again. But the most frightening development is the number of ladies accompanying their men on the club's overseas tours. This leads to all sorts of trouble with women on the tour reporting back to the girls at home what the open-side didn't do or what the No. 8 did do. The team will be robbed of good players who refuse to go on tour with the wife, or whose wife wouldn't let them go if Mrs So-And-So is going and she is to be left behind.

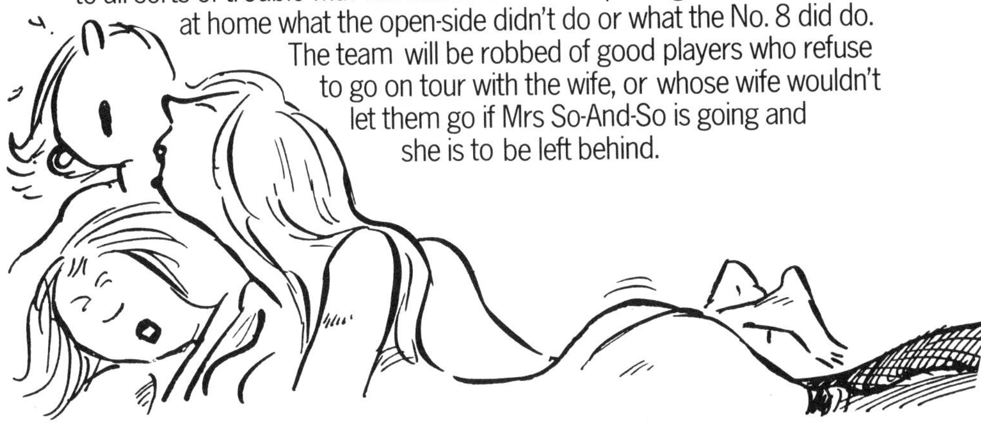

Of course, the most welcome addition to the club is the unattached young lady who just likes sport and no male in particular. Such women are still fairly thin on the ground. Meanwhile most rugby men believe that it is sensible to come to terms with the less welcome innovations and just carry on enjoying their sport – warts and all.

THE INTERNATIONAL WEEKEND

Every supporter from every country at some time or other has travelled with his own club to the big international game to cheer on his own countrymen. Whether you have come from London to Paris, from Cape Town to Johannesburg or Southland to Auckland, that long weekend is always something to remember. This is the time for building real club spirit, the time when the alickadoos and the players unite to make one happy party.

The ride to the airport is a riotous affair. Bottle corks popping, empty beer cans piling high on the card tables. The president, of all people, bursts into song with a filthy rendition. His son, the right-centre, is astounded and jumps to his feet asking his father to restrain himself.

'Shut your mouth and get that down you,' replies the president. He hands the boy a bottle. The old adage about beating them and joining them races through the boy's mind as he takes his first swig with his

father. 'That's more like it. You'll come home a better man for this weekend'.

To the airport bar and the inevitable announcement: flight delayed two hours. In which time the airport security are called on no less than six occasions and bar stocks replenished twice. With duty-free bottles under their arms and pockets full of cheap cigarettes the long walk across the tarmac is a simple task compared to the gruelling climb up the steps to the aircraft. Safely aboard and a chance to sleep. Alas no. For as soon as the eyelids touch, the outside-half slaps your head with a rolled-up newspaper.

'No sleeping on tour.'

No-one appears offended but most would appreciate a nap. The president meanwhile is playing a blinder. He has already got his son pissed and is well on the way to getting the treasurer killed by an irate husband who has been informed, quite wrongly, that the treasurer fumbled with his wife's clothing as she made her way down the aisle. The secretary, who up to now has been a popular member of the party, drops a bombshell three minutes before landing.

'Lads, I think I have left my bags at the airport'.

Generous offers of razor blades, shirts, soap and combs are forthcoming. 'No problem, Sec. We have plenty of everything between us'.

The secretary slowly says: 'Well, boys, it's like this...the match tickets were in my bag...'.

Silence. Then the first salvoes of abuse are fired. His organizational abilities are likened to the person who fails at piss-ups in breweries and bunk-ups in brothels. Then a constructive suggestion from the back of the plane:

'When we land, you get the next flight back and fetch them. All agreed?'

'Aye!'

A drunken and bemused secretary boards the next plane according to plan and the boys check into a very wreckable hotel right next door to the police station and 100 yards from the town's red-light district. In no time at all the party has become fragmented. Two of the selection committee are mugged by a dwarf in a back alley while taking a piss but are too far gone to defend themselves as the little fellow trundles off with their wallets. The whole 2nd XV pack are arrested and detained for 48 hours after heated negotiations with a brothel-keeper on the right to send in a replacement or claim a rebate should one of them fail.

In a nearby night club several members of the committee are tempted on-stage by a coloured stripper in a G-string. Within minutes they are dancing naked to a rhythmic jungle tune, hoping to impress the dusky goddess. If only the No. 8 was here! Now sweating heavily and thirsting for a drink they dance on. Then suddenly and in a cloud of smoke she disappears through a trap-door in the stage. The audience bursts forth with spontaneous and rapturous applause. The realization that their clothes have been stolen during the act does not make the applause any more acceptable than the prospect of confinement to a prison cell if they cannot borrow some fresh items of clothing. The management delve deep into their wardrobes and our heroes go out into the night air dressed as Cinderella, the two Ugly Sisters, Robin Hood and Maid Marion.

The open-side, the No. 8 and the hooker have been successful in losing Groper and Dobbin whom they consider a nuisance and a liability in their search for women. Then as they pass a dimly lit night club the sound of Groper's voice can be heard clearly singing a sentimental ballad. Upon investigation the musketeers find Seventh Heaven – a room full of lovelies and only Groper and Dobbin there to entertain them. Dawn finds

OXFAM

five of them in various stages of undress and still in the company of their new-found playmates. The morning paper carries a photograph and report of a man found face down in the gutter the previous night, brought back from the brink of death by a kiss of life from a passing ventriloquist.

'Hey, that's Bumper. Shall we go and find the hospital he's in and help him?'

The No. 8 is outraged at the suggestion. 'Do you think he would give up five birds in a bed, thirty cans of beer and a televised international to find us?'

There's no argument and the group settle into the match. The game itself is a bad example of international rugby but we scrape home, two penalties to one.

Saturday night should be the highlight of the weekend but with two helping the police in their search for a short-arsed mugger, eight in prison until Sunday morning, five in the same bed, one fighting for his life in the local infirmary and the secretary yet to arrive, the party is somewhat decimated. The president and his son walk the honky-tonks and bars uneasy in each other's company and wishing the rest of the lads could be with them.

Sunday and the flight home. Bumper is carried in a wheel-chair to the aircraft steps. The police deliver our missing pack in a large black van. The five super-studs arrive pale-faced, saggy-eyed and drawn by the weekend's activities, and the committee settle down for take-off in the same fancy dress they have been wearing all night.

Everyone has enjoyed the crack and are busy exchanging stories as the silver bird wings its way home. One or two technical problems on landing. The sight of seven men aged between thirty-five and sixty-three dressed in costumes that seemed to them so funny on Friday night does not impress the average Customs official at 1 o'clock on Sunday lunchtime. The secretary is found still scouring the airport for his bag and bundled reluctantly onto the bus for the last leg of the journey. Not to worry. It is the end of the season.

SEASON 1981-82...
HOTELS WRECKED 11,
POLICE HELMETS CAPTURED 4...
PISSED 34 TIMES,
HOPELESSLY
PISSED 52 TIMES,
DONT
REMEMBER 36 TIMES...
ARRESTED TWICE,
CHINESE RUN OUTS 17,
INDIAN —״— 19,
SENT OFF ONCE,
LEG OVERS 23...
WE'VE GOT TO DO
BETTER NEXT YEAR!